Learning from the Enemy: The GUNMAN Project

Sharon A. Maneki

**Center for Cryptologic History
National Security Agency**

2012

Cover Photo: U.S. embassy in Moscow at the time of the GUNMAN project.

Introduction

On 25 March 1985, CBS television nightly news broke the following shocking story:

- Dan Rather: "In another U.S.-Soviet development, Pentagon correspondent David Martin has been told how Soviet secret police in Moscow have been getting the latest word on sensitive U.S. embassy documents even before U.S. officials read them."

- David Martin: "Informed sources tell CBS News that for at least one year, and probably longer, the American embassy in Moscow was the victim of a sophisticated electronic spy operation which gave Soviet leaders an inside look at what U.S. diplomats were doing and planning. Soviet agents secretly installed tiny sensing devices in about a dozen embassy typewriters. The devices picked up the contents of documents typed by embassy secretaries and transmitted them by antennas hidden in the embassy walls. The antennas, in turn, relayed the signals to a listening post outside the embassy.

- "Depending on the location of the bugged typewriters, the Soviets were able to receive copies of everything from routine administrative memos to highly classified documents.

- "One intelligence officer said the potential compromise of sensitive information should be viewed with 'considerable seriousness'.

- "Another intelligence expert said no one knows for sure how many or what secrets were compromised. A third official called the entire affair a fiasco."[1]

How accurate was the CBS report? The following paper will examine the nature of the Soviet electronic penetration and the damage assessment of Soviet access to typewriters at the U.S. embassy in Moscow. This history of Project GUNMAN will also answer such questions as how the typewriter bugs were discovered and how they worked.

Countries have spied on each other by gathering information from embassies for centuries. The United States and the Soviet Union were of course archenemies during the Cold War (1945 to the fall of the Soviet Union in 1991), and there is a long history of attempts by the Soviets to gain access to information from the U.S. embassy and its diplomatic apparatus. Perhaps the most famous incident of Soviet espionage was the Great Seal implant.

On 4 August 1945, Soviet schoolchildren presented a carving of the Great Seal of the U.S. to Averell Harriman, the U.S. ambassador to the Soviet Union. The carving hung in Spaso house, the ambassador's residential office in Moscow, until 1952, when the U.S. State Department discovered that there was a microphone hidden inside the carving that the Soviets turned on at will. This bug was not a standard microphone and could not be detected unless it was in use. For six years the Soviets were able to eavesdrop on the conversations of the U.S. ambassador.[2] The Soviet threat to U.S. embassy security was both well documented and real.

The typewriter bugs marked a new level of sophistication because they were electromechanical. For the first time, the Soviets gathered information from a piece of equipment that held written plain text information. Prior to the discovery of these bugs, the U.S. believed that the Russians had only used room audio bugs with microphones or listening devices to eavesdrop on American embassy activities. As a totalitarian society, the Soviet Union valued eavesdropping and thus developed ingenious methods to accomplish it.

The 1980s were a period of strained relations between the U.S. and the Soviet Union. One manifestation of those strains was Project GUNMAN, which involved the replacement of U.S. embassy equipment in Moscow and the discovery and evaluation of typewriter bugs. GUNMAN was not the only threat to the U.S. embassy in Moscow. The U.S. began to build a new office for its Moscow embassy in 1979. The building, however, was riddled with bugs, and the U.S. eventually rejected it. That story is a subject for another study. This study is the story of the GUNMAN attack and the role of NSA in its discovery.

Organizations with intelligence responsibilities must be able to respond quickly and creatively to unforeseen threats. How did NSA respond to this Soviet threat? To answer that question, this monograph will examine the role of NSA leadership and its ability to move a bureaucracy into action. To curtail future threats, intelligence organizations must also maintain the ability to learn from the activities of their enemies. What techniques did NSA use to learn from Soviet bugging efforts?

The Catalyst

The CBS 25 March 1985 report that announced to the world that the Soviets had penetrated typewriters in the U.S. embassy in Moscow was correct in that the attack took place. According to CBS, "the bugs might still be in place had it not been for a warning from a friendly government whose own embassy had been the target of a similar eavesdropping operation."[3]

After learning about the bug at the foreign embassy in August 1983, the Director of NSA (DIRNSA), Lt. General Lincoln Faurer, sent analysts from R9, the Research and Development organization, and from the Communications Security (COMSEC) organization to examine the implant the other nation had discovered. It was unusual for the Research and COMSEC organizations to have a reason to work together. This was the first of many examples of collaboration that developed between the two entities to uncover and understand the GUNMAN threat.

The analysts found that this implant (which would prove to be very different from the ones later found in the U.S. embassy) represented a major Soviet technological improvement over their previous efforts. The development of this bug required competent personnel, time, and money. The very manufacture of the components required a massive and modern infrastructure serviced by many people. This combination of resources led to the assumption that other units were available.[4]

The bug, which was not in typewriters but in other types of equipment, could be rapidly and easily installed by nontechnical personnel; it resisted detection by conventional methods; and it was wireless and remotely controlled. Search by disassembly and visual inspection, when conducted by any but the best-trained technicians, would normally be unproductive. All concluded that if the Soviet KGB would go to these lengths against a Western ally, then certainly the United States could expect to be a high-priority target.[5] The warning was the catalyst for NSA action.

Under the leadership of Walter Deeley, the deputy director for communication security, and the chief of R9, a division in the Research and Development organization, NSA management developed a plan to remove, replace, and examine telecommunications and information processing equipment at the U.S. embassy in Moscow.

NSA was to handle all aspects of the plan on an absolutely need-to-know basis. NSA wanted to remove all of the equipment so that it could be examined in the U.S. to allow for a more thorough inspection than could be conducted on the embassy grounds. NSA also wanted to keep the Soviet Union from learning about the effort and interfering with U.S. objectives. The Soviets had a history of poisoning or using other means to injure technicians from other countries who investigated bugs in their respective embassies.[6]

General Faurer did not want to bring this plan to the State Department because relations between NSA and State were poor. NSA had been writing critical reports about inadequate security in State Department facilities for several years. Faurer also believed that CIA would mishandle the NSA plan.[7]

NSA briefed the secretary of defense, Caspar Weinberger, on the threat of a possible bug in U.S. embassy equipment and its proposed plan of action. Weinberger said that this problem should be brought to the attention of the president immediately. The individual whom Deeley assigned to work with the White House later explained that the approval from President Reagan for the NSA plan of action came in record time.

I briefed Ken DeGraffenreid [the senior director of intelligence programs on the National Security Council]. Next we briefed Admiral John Poindexter [the deputy national security adviser, who became the national security adviser in 1985]. Admiral Poindexter wrote the necessary memorandum and within a few days we had a signed document of authorization from the president.

President Reagan approved the GUNMAN project in February 1984.

Even after presidential approval, knowledge of GUNMAN was still tightly held within the government. The individual further explained:

Admiral Poindexter told me to brief the secretary of state [George Schultz] and the director of Central Intelligence [William Casey], and no one else. I pleaded to brief Lawrence Eagleburger [under-secretary for political affairs], because I feared that I could not reach the secretary of state if we needed help in gaining the cooperation of the State Department. After much begging, Poindexter relented. This incident is an indication of the concern for security within the U.S. government.[8]

Developing in just a few months a detailed plan for removing, replacing, and examining every piece of telecommunications and information processing equipment at the Moscow embassy, and getting presidential approval to proceed, was a significant achievement. This was a testament to the leadership of Walter Deeley, a manager who took risks and made decisions. Right from the start of GUNMAN, the research and COMSEC directorates worked together. This type of collaboration was very effective but a very unusual phenomenon in the 1980s. Overcoming bureaucratic hurdles was also possible because during the 1980s the Reagan administration had an overarching concern with the Soviet threat to the U.S.

The Race to Remove
and Replace Embassy Equipment

The first goal of the GUNMAN Project, to replace all of the electronic equipment in the U.S. embassy in Moscow with signaturized equipment, was a daunting challenge. Electronic equipment included teletype machines, printers, computers, cryptographic devices, and copiers – in short, almost anything that plugged into a wall socket. NSA staff had to move quickly to replace equipment to avoid tipping off the Soviets. According to an analyst who was involved with the procurement and shipment of the upgraded equipment to Moscow, Walter Deeley gave the staff one hundred days to complete this phase of the project. The analyst stated,

> *The first problem that we faced was the lack of a centralized inventory at the embassy. The problem was further complicated because individual departments had software tailored to their specific needs. For instance, we could not simply replace all of the Wang computers. Keeping track of all of the various software was hard enough, but keeping track of all of the variations was a nightmare. With the assistance of a few trusted communication center embassy employees, we were able to obtain diagrams and blueprints of equipment. However, we found that frequently the original diagram did not always match with the equipment that had been actually delivered.*

Security concerns were another challenge identified by the NSA technicians.

> *We could not simply show up to take an inventory because we could not risk alerting the Soviets. Instead, telecommunication personnel from NSA were sent to the embassy. They quickly obtained the information that we needed to procure the necessary equipments.*[9]

NSA used a variety of methods to quickly purchase similar or upgraded equipment for the embassy. Approximately 40 percent of the equipment had to be purchased while 60 percent was available from the Agency and other sources. NSA was unable to obtain 250 IBM Selectric typewriters required by the embassy in part because of their power requirement. The Soviet Union used 220-volt 60-cycle electricity. Typewriters were not available from European sources, and the IBM factory in Lexington, Kentucky, had depleted most of its stock. NSA was able to acquire only fifty typewriters, so they replaced typewriters that were used in the most sensitive areas of the embassy. NSA was able to meet the requirements for all other equipment.[10]

Because of the need for fast delivery to the embassy once the equipment arrived in Moscow, NSA had to be certain that each piece of equipment worked. There would be no time to repair anything. NSA also wanted to make sure that the replacement equipment was not tampered with while en route. The COMSEC organization took a number of steps not only to safeguard the equipment in transit, but also to determine whether it was tampered with when it was brought back for periodic examination after being operational in the field. For the next two months, personnel primarily from S65 (COMSEC Standards and Advanced Technology Division) and T2 (Technology Directorate) worked feverishly to prepare the equipment for shipment. This was another example of collaboration between organizations within NSA.

A separate area on the NSAW campus, known as the T Motor Pool area, contained four trailers that were used to stage the equipment. T2 used the first trailer to test each piece of equipment to ensure its proper function. In the second trailer, COMSEC personnel inspected each item by x-ray. They also disassembled every item to record anomalies that would be stored in their standards library for future reference during examination when the equipment came back from the field. They performed special procedures in the third trailer and used the last one for storage.

Every possible precaution was taken during the entire project to ensure that the replacement equipment remained secure. NSA staff guarded against tampering by using several levels of detection devices. Some methods were applied to the equipment itself, while others involved the packaging of the equipment. Personnel used various tamper-proof methods to package the equipment. For example, equipment was sealed in special plastic bags that could not be replicated in the Soviet Union. Some boxes contained special equipment. To the best of NSA's knowledge, the Soviets did not interfere with any of the equipment that was shipped to the embassy or returned to Fort Meade.[11]

The staff took extraordinary measures to ensure the security of the equipment during its shipment to the embassy. In preparation for shipment, boxes of equipment were placed in crates which were wrapped in burlap. Burlap signified that these items were to be treated as U.S. diplomatic cargo and would not be subject to inspection by Soviet customs officials. As a further security measure, the burlap was stapled onto each crate. Next, the crates were placed in trailers for easier transport and additional security.

From NSA, the Armed Forces Courier Service shipped the equipment to Dover Air Force Base. An example of attention to every detail of security was the rental of a special crane to load the plane. The regular crane was not operational when the equipment arrived. The flight was scheduled to leave in three hours. The equipment could not miss that flight because NSA personnel did not want to store it at Dover. Therefore, the plane was loaded using a rented crane.

Two cleared couriers accompanied the equipment, which was flown by military transport to Frankfurt, Germany. The equipment was stored and guarded by U.S. personnel at a warehouse in Germany until it could be flown into Moscow. This was necessary because there was no place at the embassy to store ten tons of equipment. The embassy attic had been damaged in a fire in 1978 and was not stable enough to hold such heavy equipment.

The equipment was flown into Moscow in stages on a Lufthansa aircraft, a common State Department procedure. The Soviets were not surprised by an influx of equipment entering the embassy because such activity was typical in the spring. The only way to get equipment into the embassy was by using a hoist from the outside. This hoist was frozen all winter and inoperable, making larger deliveries necessary in the spring. However, the Soviets did turn off the electricity to the embassy elevator for preventive maintenance after the first day of the influx of equipment. Most of the approximately ten tons of equipment that went into the embassy and the eleven tons that came out had to be carried manually. (Note: Some sources maintain that less equipment went into the embassy as replacements because the equipments were upgraded models. Other sources maintain that eleven tons came out of the embassy because there were bags of sensitive trash that NSA wanted to examine back at Fort Meade.)

The true nature of the GUNMAN project was successfully masked from most embassy employees. Ambassador Arthur Hartman learned about the project via a handwritten note that NSA personnel personally delivered when they arrived at the embassy. Ambassador Hartman announced that there was to be an upgrade of embassy

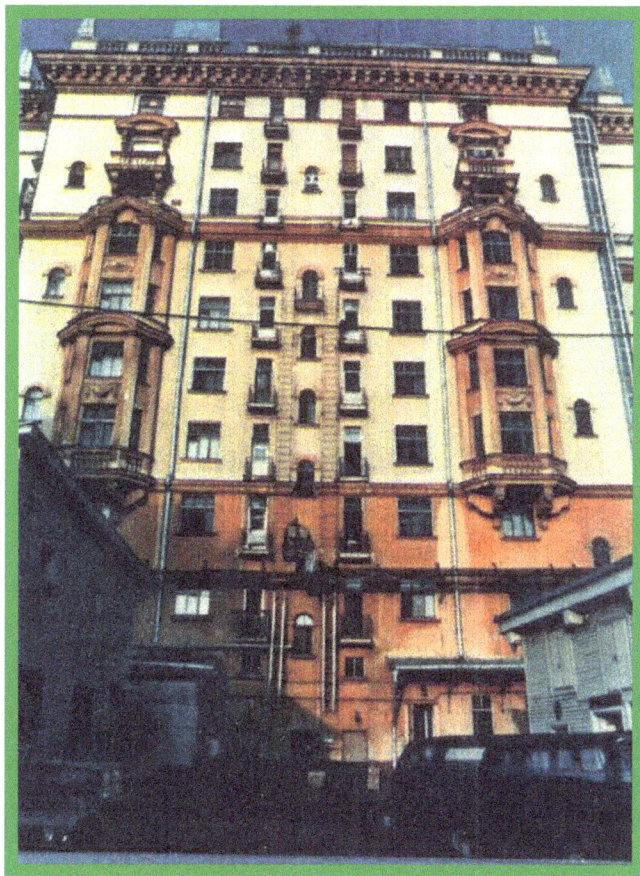

Fig. 1. U.S. embassy in Moscow. Equipment was lifted in and out of this building, possibly from the roof, since the Soviets had shut down the elevator.

communications, which accounted for all of the replaced equipment.[12] Embassy personnel were happy because they received new equipment and upgrades without having to use any of their own funding.[13]

The embassy environment made the swap of equipment even more difficult. A State Department employee who was the deputy chief of the communications center at the Moscow embassy, described the facility as old, decrepit, and outdated. As an employee in the U.S. Foreign Service, he had worked in many facilities in similar shape throughout the world. He reported that it was difficult to move equipment around because the halls were only thirty-six inches wide and the elevator could hold only four passengers, never mind equipment. The only way to get some equipment moved was to manually haul it up and down the stairs. The embassy employee further stated,

> *I did not mind the rugged working conditions or long hours because I was accustomed to it from other embassy work. Every embassy is at the mercy of the host country because it must depend on the host for water, electricity and heat just as any other building in a country is dependent on that country for utilities. It was more difficult in Moscow because we had an adversarial relationship. Sometimes the Soviets played games by shutting off utilities.[14]*

The head of the State Department communication center at the Moscow embassy, further described the atmosphere at the embassy as very intense. Nobody trusted the Soviets.

> *Workers took their jobs seriously. We were always under the watchful eye of the Soviets, even in our personal life. I lived in an apartment outside the U.S. compound. I would come home to find my freezer unplugged, shirts missing from my closet, or a dirty glass in the sink that had contained liquor. I am sure that the apartment was bugged. Americans had no privacy.[15]*

The replacement of all of the embassy electronic equipment had to occur with minimal impact on the mission. An NSA employee who was sent to the U.S. embassy in Moscow to carry out the replacement of the equipment described the activities as follows:

I arrived late on a Saturday and began work early on Sunday morning. I had two kinds of tasks, protect the equipment that was held overnight in the attic and help with the unloading and loading of equipment. I brought alarms and sensors that I set up in the attic. I ran the wires down to the Marine guards on the sixth floor. No one interfered with our equipment while we were there.

The logistics of the operation were handled superbly. A shipping clerk was part of the team. He opened the diplomatic pouch, uncrated the equipment and opened the box. We carried the equipment down to its position. While members of the team set up the new piece of equipment, others brought the old one back to the attic where it was repackaged in the box that contained the new equipment. We spent lots of time running up and down the stairs. The teletype machines were really, really heavy. They were also very wide and could barely fit through the stairways.

We started changing equipment in the State Department communication center. We systematically worked our way through the rest of the building. I was at the embassy for ten days. It was a real adventure.[16]

The exchange of equipment between NSA and the U.S. embassy in Moscow was another example of overcoming bureaucratic delays. NSA personnel demonstrated a tremendous capacity for hard work. They also exhibited deep dedication to the mission.

The Discovery

Since S65 was an office that handled a wide variety of special projects, it was appropriate to give this division the lead in looking for bugs in U.S. equipment. The head of this division reported that he pulled together a team of the best minds to work on this challenging task. This assignment was an unusual one for NSA. The division chief was careful to assign the "right number of people to the task. I did not want people stumbling over each other and getting in each other's way. We needed space for people to do their work. Too many people would have created confusion. I did not want them inadvertently missing anything."[17]

As the equipment from the embassy was returned to NSA, the COMSEC organization began a lengthy inspection process of each item. The equipment had to be inspected methodically to prevent the destruction of important evidence. The accountable COMSEC equipment was examined in the labs inside the OPS-3 or S building, the COMSEC facility on Fort Meade, while the nonaccountable COMSEC equipment was stored and examined in the trailers. Each item was inspected visually and then x-rayed. The x-rays were compared with known standards for each item.[18]

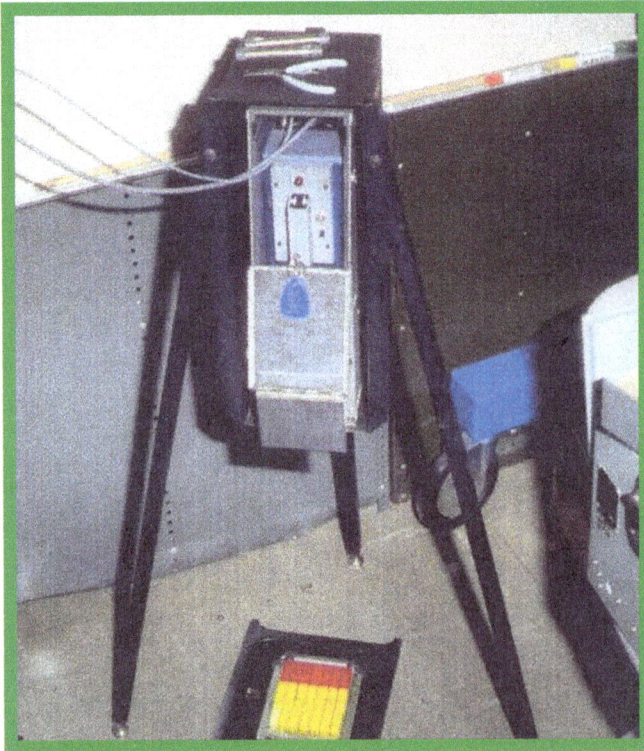

Fig. 2. Primary x-ray machine used in detecting equipment bugs. This was a portable machine about 8 inches deep, 6 inches wide, and 12-15 inches long. It was pointed at the floor when taking an x-ray; a sheet of x-ray film was placed under the item.

A physicist who worked in S65 described the atmosphere as the search for bugs proceeded at NSA:

The adrenalin was really flowing. About twenty-five of us were involved in the search. We all recognized the importance of our work. NSA's reputation was on the line, and it was up to us to find something. We felt sure that the Soviets were taking advantage of us.

We worked six days a week and did not even complain about rough working conditions. When we started working in the trailers, there were no steps up to the entrance. The entrance was about four feet off the ground. We found some cinder blocks and empty spools that had contained mesh wire to help us enter the trailer. Eventually we got steps, phones, and air conditioning, and life improved.[19]

Walter Deeley had a long, varied career at the Agency. He had a reputation for being strong willed, abrasive, but committed to the mission. Directors of the Agency turned to him when they needed someone to accomplish a difficult job. As the head of the COMSEC organization, Deeley wanted the question of whether the Soviets were bugging U.S. equipment answered quickly. He demonstrated his impatience by swapping managers for the project in midstream.[20] He also offered a $5,000 bonus to the person who found a bug.[21]

An engineering technician in S65 who was working on this project enjoyed the challenge of searching for a bug in U.S. equipment. According to him, the 1980s were a time when people felt patriotism and pride in their country.

We knew who the enemy was and wanted to limit his effect. I frequently worked at night and on the weekends by myself in the trailer examining equipment. After we had looked at all of the crypto gear, we eventually made our way to examining the typewriters. I took a typewriter apart to look at all of the possible places where a bug could be inserted. I created an image of these areas which enabled me to take fewer but clearer x-rays of the important sections.[22]

On a Monday evening, 23 July, a technician noticed an extra coil on the power switch of an IBM Selectric typewriter. He decided to x-ray the whole machine from top to bottom. The x-rays of the keyboard proved to be very interesting:[23]

> *When I saw those x-rays, my response was 'holy f***'. They really were bugging our equipment. I was very excited, but no one was around to tell the news. My wife was an NSA employee, but I could not even tell her because of the level of classification of the project. I could hardly wait for morning when my colleagues would return.[24]*

He continued the story:

> *The next morning, [engineers] argued about whether we had an anomaly or a bugged typewriter. Some typewriters had memory now which could account for additional circuits. What led us to conclude that this typewriter was probably bugged was the location of so many circuits in a metal bar that went along the length of the machine. When our boss arrived, we informed him and he called in other experts from R9. Deeley informed the DIRNSA. Now the pace of our work really increased. We had to thoroughly examine all embassy typewriters in the USSR because most likely there were more bugs. We had to educate other U.S. embassy personnel from East Bloc countries on how to search for bugs. We also began the difficult task of reverse engineering the bug to see how it worked. I had been discouraging the wide use of x-rays because we had difficulty obtaining Polaroid film. Polaroid only made about 3,000 sheets of film a year. We had used 10,000 sheets and were having trouble obtaining film. Thank goodness [my advice was ignored] and the entire machine was x-rayed. There was no way to see that bug without x-rays.[25]*

The technician who discovered the implant claimed to have no special talent:

> *I found that bug by luck. After looking at so many x-rays day after day for so many hours, I could easily have missed it. I'm glad that I saw it. I certainly was delighted with the $5,000 cash award.[26]*

Another technician believed that the GUNMAN experience had an important positive effect on the COMSEC organization:

> *Another lesson that GUNMAN taught us was to expand our thinking. Many of us in the COMSEC area expected the bug to be in crypto or other COMSEC equipment. It ended up being in a typewriter that produced plain text. We had to pay more attention to plain text communication devices if we were to keep U.S. communications secure.*[27]

Reactions to the GUNMAN Find

One technician characterized the reaction to the GUNMAN find within the organizations that had worked on the project as chaotic. "Everyone jumped on the bandwagon and wanted to take credit for the find. Everyone wanted to be on stage. S65 was pushed into the background. Deeley handpicked the people to brief President Reagan at the White House. R9 grabbed publicity, too."[28] As Count Galeazzo Ciano summed up human nature in his diary in World War II, "As always, victory finds a hundred fathers but defeat is an orphan."

The discovery that the Soviets had bugged a typewriter in the U.S. embassy in Moscow did not diminish the level of secrecy surrounding the GUNMAN project. A technical writer in S64, the Tempest office,[29] which was located next to S65, saw large amounts of equipment going up and down the hall. She even helped with the procurement of film and packaging materials. She learned about the true nature of the GUNMAN project only after the implant was discovered. Even then her supervisor swore her to keep the information secret.

One morning, with no time for preparation, she was told to brief the deputy director, Robert Rich, on the GUNMAN implant. She did the best she could with the briefing, but determined that she would learn as much as possible about the subject. Since the engineers were very busy with their investigations, she soon became the NSA GUNMAN briefer.

While the search for additional bugs continued, the secrecy of GUNMAN remained paramount. The technical writer briefed Agency seniors about GUNMAN. People were briefed one at a time in an anechoic chamber, a soundproof anti-echo room used to conduct technical tests. She reported that the reaction to the news ranged from astonishment to anger.

Over time, the need to warn others of the Soviet threat grew, and NSA began to brief other members of the intelligence community. Balancing the need for secrecy versus the need to warn against a threat was a difficult task. The writer briefed the GUNMAN project for seven years. One of the highlights for her was briefing the President's Foreign Intelligence Advisory Board. Normally this task would fall to Agency seniors, but none were available so she was able to go to the White House to make the presentation.[30] Other analysts who also worked in S64 reported that a GUNMAN briefing team went on the road to warn U.S. allies of the Soviet threat. Some members of the team gave presentations and some answered technical questions from the audience.[31]

In 1985, when the story of the Soviet bug of U.S. typewriters in the Moscow embassy broke on the CBS nightly news, William Casey, the director of the Central Intelligence Agency, was furious. He demanded a list of everyone that NSA had briefed on the GUNMAN project. The technical writer was glad that she was able to supply that list. Casey eventually dropped the investigation of the leak because the task of discovery was impossible. Too many people knew about GUNMAN.[32]

Implant Characteristics

A discussion arose within the COMSEC organization about whether the GUNMAN bug should be reverse engineered by a contractor or by the organization itself. Some engineers insisted that they had the capability to do this work. One had gained reverse engineering experience at a previous job with Naval Intelligence.[33] Management sided with the engineers, and reverse engineering of the GUNMAN bug became an in-house project. This was an important decision because it enabled NSA to learn a great deal about the ingenuity of the Soviets and to gain a better understanding of the threat. This decision also showed that management and subordinates had a good working relationship and that subordinates had initiative. It was an atmosphere that furthered the Agency's ability to fully carry out its mission.

NSA analysts left no stone unturned in reverse engineering the implant. The COMSEC and Research organizations devoted considerable time and effort into studying all aspects of the bug. NSA was determined to learn from the enemy. As the following discussion demonstrates, reverse engineering was very successful. Analysts uncovered numerous characteristics of the implant.

A brief explanation of the general characteristics of IBM Selectric typewriters will aid in the understanding of how the implant worked. Most typewriters had metal arms that swung up against a ribbon to type a letter. IBM Selectrics, however, were unique because they used a round ball with numbers and letters around the outside surface. When a typist struck a key, the ball moved into position over an inked plastic ribbon and descended to imprint the character onto the paper.

Fig. 3. IBM Selectric typewriter

The lot of equipment from the U.S. embassy in Moscow that was shipped back to NSA contained forty-four typewriters, six of which were bugged. The first step in evaluating the implant was to compare a bugged with a nonbugged typewriter. As S65 and R9 personnel disassembled the typewriters side by side, they took video and still photography of each part to ensure a thorough evaluation. Some of the unique characteristics of bugged typewriters were that these typewriters had an additional spring lug and screw; had a modified switch; and had modified bails (the official term for bail is interpose latch) or arms that controlled the pitch and rotation of the ball.

Reverse engineering was another example of how entities within NSA worked in collaboration even though they were in different organizations. Personnel from S65 and R9 divided the reverse engineering tasks. R9 personnel focused on the operational aspects of the bug. S65 personnel removed the printed wire assemblies and determined the emanation capabilities. Together, S65 and R9 personnel drew logic diagrams describing the circuits. S65 personnel also trained people from other agencies to perform visual and x-ray inspections of equipment in the field so that they could look for bugs. This training paid off because seven additional typewriters in the Moscow embassy and three typewriters in the Leningrad consulate contained implants. A total of sixteen bugs were found in twelve IBM Selectric II typewriters and four IBM Selectric III typewriters. Common features were found in all sixteen typewriters: six ferromagnetic magnetizable bails were replaced with six nonferromagnetic nonmagnetizable bails with a very strong magnet in the tip; all the typewriters contained a modified comb support bar which housed the bug; all used burst transmissions at the 30, 60, or 90 MHZ range via radio frequency.

The Soviets continually upgraded and improved their implants. There were five varieties or generations of bugs. Three types of units operated using DC power and contained either eight, nine, or ten batteries. The other two types operated from AC power and had beacons to indicate whether the typewriter was turned on or off. Some of the units also had a modified on and off switch with a transformer, while others had a special coaxial screw with a spring and lug. The modified switch sent power to the implant. Since the battery-powered machines had their own internal source of power, the modified switch was not necessary. The special coaxial screw with a spring and lug connected the implant to the typewriter linkage, and this linkage was used as an antenna to transmit the information as it was being typed.[34] Later battery-powered implants had a test point underneath an end screw. By removing the screw and inserting a probe, an individual could easily read battery voltage to see if the batteries were still active.

The ingenuity of the Soviets was remarkable because they did not merely move from batteries as a source of power to alternating current. There were early versions and later versions of bugs that used both sources of power. NSA found that the first three implants were battery powered. The first of these was shipped to Moscow in October 1976, and the other two were shipped in April of 1977. The first bug that used alternating current as its source of power was shipped to Moscow in November 1977. The remaining nine machines that were found in Moscow used alternating current as their source of power and were more advanced than the first AC-powered bug. Five of the advanced model AC bugged typewriters were delivered to Moscow in February 1982. The remainder were delivered in January of 1984.[35] The later battery-powered bugged typewriters found in the consulate in Leningrad were shipped in April of 1977 and March of 1982.[36]

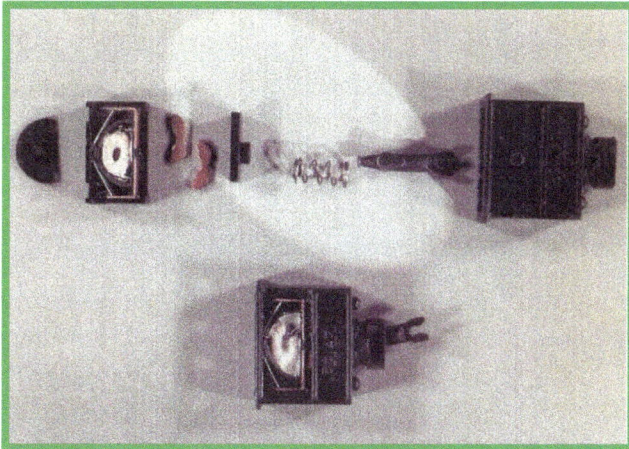

Fig. 4. Exploded views of bugged power switch

All of the implants were quite sophisticated. Each implant had a magnetometer that converted the mechanical energy of key strokes into local magnetic disturbances. The electronics package in the implant responded to these disturbances, categorized the underlying data, and transmitted the results to a nearby listening post. Data were transmitted via radio frequency. The implant was enabled by remote control.[37] Another advantage of these bugs was easy installation. Engineers estimated that a skilled technician could install an implant in a typewriter in a half hour.[38] The integrated circuits were very sophisticated for that time period. The circuits contained one bit core memory, an advancement that NSA engineers had never seen.[39]

When the press learned that the Soviets were bugging typewriters in the U.S. embassy in 1985, reporters tried to describe the characteristics of these bugs. One of the more technical explanations appeared in the June 1985 edition of *Discover* magazine. How accurate was that description?

In an article entitled "Tapping the Keys," a bugging expert offered the following explanation of the Soviet bug:

> *The Soviets must have taken advantage of the way the Selectric types. A metal ball covered with characters spins so that the appropriate character strikes the paper and then spins back to its starting point. The time it takes to accomplish the rotation to each letter is different. A low-tech listening device planted in the room could transmit the sounds of a typing Selectric to a computer. The computer could then easily measure the time intervals between each key stroke and the character being put on the paper, and thus determine which character had been tapped.*[40]

An engineer in the COMSEC organization who was involved in reverse engineering the GUNMAN bug explained that the press had a good idea, but it was inaccurate: "IBM Selectric typewriters used a spinning ball to get the right character on the paper. The bug was not based on sound or timing." He further elaborated: "The Soviets were very good with metal. Housing the bug in a metal bar was ingenious. The bar was difficult to open and it really concealed the bug from inspection."[41] Another engineer from R9 who also worked on this project agreed:

> *To the naked eye, the bar looked like a single unit. You could not see that it could be opened. The use of low power and short transmission bursts also made it*

difficult to detect this bug. The bug contained integrated circuits that were very advanced for that time period. The implant was really very sophisticated.[42]

The discovery of this bug by NSA technicians was a significant technical achievement.

The press did not understand the level of sophistication of the GUNMAN bug. For instance, an article from *Time* magazine speculated "the Soviets somehow encoded the machine's typing function, giving each character a distinguishing electronic or magnetic signature."[43]

In reality, the movement of the bails determined which character had been typed because each character had a unique binary movement corresponding to the bails. The magnetic energy picked up by the sensors in the bar was converted into a digital electrical signal. The signals were compressed into a four-bit frequency select word. The bug was able to store up to eight four-bit characters. When the buffer was full, a transmitter in the bar sent the information out to Soviet sensors.

There was some ambiguity in determining which characters had been typed. NSA analysts using the laws of probability were able to figure out how the Soviets probably recovered text. Other factors which made it difficult to recover text included the following: The implant could not detect characters that were typed without the ball moving. If the typist pressed space, tab shift, or backspace, these characters were invisible to the implant. Since the ball did not move or tilt when the typist pressed hyphen because it was located at the ball's home position, the bug could not read this character either.[44]

Damage Assessment

Despite the ambiguities in knowing what characters were typed, the typewriter attack against the U.S. was a lucrative source of information for the Soviets. It was difficult to quantify the damage to the U.S. from this exploitation because it went on for such a long time. The FBI examined typewriter inventory records to determine when the sixteen bugged machines arrived at the Moscow embassy and the Leningrad consulate, where the typewriters were located in each facility, and to whom they were assigned. The FBI was unable to uncover the answers to these questions for several reasons. The State Department had a policy at both the embassy and consulate of routinely destroying records every two years. State Department personnel normally rotate to new assignments every two years so responsibility for procurement of typewriters and inventory controls and maintenance changed frequently. There was no continuity of procedures for inventory control.[45]

A Cunning Enemy

Why did the U.S. fail to detect bugs in its typewriters for so long? One of the main reasons the bugs remained undetected for approximately eight years was that the U.S. used outdated and inappropriate techniques and equipment when conducting inspections and made mistakes in analysis. Another important reason was that the Soviets proved to be a cunning enemy. Much of the equipment used by U.S. Technical Security Countermeasure (TSCM) teams dated back to the 1950s. The GUNMAN device used burst transmissions that were so short the signal disappeared from the spectrum before it could be recognized by the older spectrum analyzers used by the TSCM teams. Burst transmissions also occurred intermittently due to the speed of the typist. Since the devices were remotely controlled, the Soviets could turn them off when inspection teams were in the area. Newer spectrum analyzers had memory and could integrate energy detected over a period of time. Newer analyzers may have detected the GUNMAN device, but there would have to have been an element of luck. When using the spectrum analyzer, the typewriter would have to have been turned on, the bug would have to have been on, and the analyzer would have to have been tuned to the right frequency range.

The design of the GUNMAN bar indicated that the Soviets had knowledge of techniques used by American TSCM teams when inspecting facilities. For instance, the Soviets must have known that the U.S. used nonlinear detectors because the GUNMAN device was designed to filter out frequency harmonics, which is an integral part of what a nonlinear detector is searching for. The Soviets also used snuggling techniques to hide the transmission of the bug in the noise of the transmission of television stations. They deliberately set the devices in the same frequency band as their television stations so that U.S. analyzers would miss the transmissions.

Once the GUNMAN bug was discovered, it became clear that some U.S. analysts had misinterpreted clues over the years. In 1978 inspectors found an antenna in the chimney in the U.S. embassy in Moscow. The intelligence community was never able to figure out the purpose of that antenna. Typewriters were examined in 1978, but the technician did not find any bugs. The technician assumed that if a modification had been made to a typewriter it would be in the power structure. Therefore, he took x-rays of only the start capacitor and switch and the motor. In 1978 the source of power for the implants was batteries so no changes were made to the power structure of the typewriter. Technicians missed the bugs. Despite these indications of Soviet exploitation of typewriters, the U.S. Department of State took no action to protect its typewriters.[46]

The Soviets exercised great caution with their own electric typewriters. They prohibited their staff from using electric typewriters for classified information. Manual typewriters that were to be used for the processing of classified information were to be shipped from Moscow to other Soviet embassies only in diplomatic pouches. When these typewriters were not in use at the various embassies, they were to be stored in sealed containers.[47]

Some consolation from the U.S. perspective was that there was no indication that a U.S. person was involved in the GUNMAN attack. The implant devices were most likely installed by the Soviet Intelligence Service when the typewriters were under the control of Soviet customs officials before they reached their destination at the embassy or consulate.[48] These facts do not diminish the ingenuity and determination of the Soviets. As General Faurer explained in 1986:

> *I think people tend to fall into the trap of being disdainful too often of their adversaries. Recently, we*

tended to think that in technical matters we were ahead of the Soviet Union—for example in computers, aircraft engines, cars. In recent years, we have encountered surprise after surprise and are more respectful. Most folks would now concede that they have enormously narrowed the gap and have caught us in a number of places.[49]

GUNMAN Impact

The GUNMAN project had a major impact on the intelligence community as a whole. It brought about a greater understanding of the thinking and operations in a totalitarian society. The community became more aware of the hostile electronic threat against the U.S. as NSA briefed all levels of government to warn of the danger. NSA was not out to assess blame; it took the problem-solving approach.[50]

When the GUNMAN story broke in the press, the State Department was forced to take security more seriously. The Bureau of Diplomatic Security of the U.S. State Department and its Diplomatic Security Service (DSS) were established officially on 4 November 1985. This bureau's purview covered all aspects of the security needs for the department, for its facilities at home and abroad, and for its employees and their families. The importance of the new organization was indicated by making its head an assistant secretary of state.[51]

Numerous panels were formed to investigate not only how and why the Soviets were able to bug embassy typewriters, but also all areas of embassy security. These panels made numerous recommendations. Only some of the recommendations were implemented due to a lack of cooperation between the various segments of the intelligence community. The congressional committees on intelligence oversight threatened to reorganize the technical security countermeasures organizations within the various agencies to bring about coordination and reduce duplication of effort. To avoid this type of congressional action, the Intelligence Community formed the Senior Interagency Group for Intelligence. This body attempted to get the agencies to work together, but they found it difficult to share information with each other. The CIA and the FBI, however, did reorganize and upgrade their technical security organizations.[52]

GUNMAN had a long-term positive effect on the State Department's policies and procedures for shipping plain text processing equipment. In 1988 the State Department built a facility to inspect and package all plain text processing equipment that is shipped overseas. This facility is still in operation today. The Department also maintains a list of preferred items that will enhance security.[53] In comparison to the rest of the intelligence community, many people believe that the State Department has the best security measures today for protecting unclassified equipment that is shipped abroad.

GUNMAN also had some positive effects on NSA. As an engineer in the research and development organization during the time of GUNMAN explained:

> *Before 1984 the community did not believe NSA and its abilities. As a result of the 1984 work on GUNMAN, the stature of NSA in terms of dealing with the embassy security community changed radically. We became the voice to listen to, and I'm very proud of that.*[54]

Plans that had been stalled were implemented because of GUNMAN. For instance, the National Security Council promulgated National Security Decision Directive (NSDD) 145. This directive, signed on 17 September 1984, made DIRNSA the national manager for telecommunications and automation information systems security.[55]

After the GUNMAN revelations, several changes came about within the COMSEC organization at NSA. While the GUNMAN discovery was not the only cause for these changes, it certainly influenced their implementation. In 1985 the name of the COMSEC organization was changed to the Information Security (INFOSEC) organization.[56] Information security denoted an expansion of responsibilities for the organization. The organization had more to protect than just the transmission of information. This name change also reflected the greater awareness of the need to protect plain text information and the intention of the Deputy Director for Information Systems Security (DDI) to place greater emphasis on the protection of plain text. NSA management reorganized the INFOSEC organization to better handle its information security responsibilities. For instance, the organization became more involved in technical security countermeasures. The Technical Security Engineering Center, X3, created on 14 May 1986, became responsible for advanced technology development, fabrication security–the security of equipment as it is being built–technical security, and facility evaluation. Plans called for X3 and R9, which were responsible for the exploitation of the adversary's communications, to jointly conduct facility evaluations. NSA hoped to improve technical security through this more coordinated approach.57

In the late 1970s an expert from CIA came to NSA to start an anti-tamper technology program. In the spring of 1984, when NSA sent replacement equipment to the Moscow embassy, NSA had its own program to protect keying material and equipment, but it was small in comparison to the CIA program.

Because of the GUNMAN revelations and other compromises, such as the Walker spy ring,58 NSA expanded its anti-tamper program. Customers were more receptive to using these solutions because they recognized the security threat. Technicians at NSA invented new anti-tamper technologies such as holograph and prism labels that could not be easily duplicated by an adversary who tried to remove them from a package.59

On 1 May 1989, in recognition of both the growth and importance of these technologies, the INFOSEC organization consolidated all of its anti-tamper programs into a new separate division, Y26, the Protective Technologies Implementation Division.60 In recognition of the need to train customers in the proper use of tamper technologies, a separate awareness and education branch was established within the division. Prior to the formation of this branch, technologies were provided to the customer without any emphasis on their proper use. A chemist who worked in various technology tamper programs reported on a visit she made to see a customer on the USS *Witman* in the spring of 1984:

> *I asked the COMSEC custodian where he stored the keying material. He showed me the plastic bags that had contained a tamper-proof canister. He praised the use of the plastic bags and said they were great for storing fish bait. To my horror, the fellow was removing all of the key from the canister which was intended for key storage. Instead of removing only the key needed for that day, he was taking it out all at once, which totally eliminated the tamper protection. Without training, what could we expect?* [61]

Corrective actions were taken and because of its anti-tamper program, NSA became a leader in technical security.

Conclusions

From approximately 1976 to 1984, the Soviet Union used electromechanical implants to gather information from typewriters located in the U.S. embassy in Moscow and the U.S. consulate in Leningrad. Project GUNMAN was NSA's plan to remove communications and information processing equipment from the U.S. embassy in Moscow and bring it back to Fort Meade. Phase two of the project was to thoroughly examine each piece of equipment in search of a bug. GUNMAN was well planned and well executed. Within five months ten tons of equipment was procured and delivered to the embassy without interruption to embassy operations. Eleven tons of equipment was brought back to Fort Meade, and the first bug was discovered on 24 July 1984. NSA managers were able to move a large bureaucracy into action to meet a major threat to U.S. security. The actual discovery of the bug demonstrated the talent of NSA technicians.

Eight months after the GUNMAN discovery, the story broke in the press. By highlighting the damage, press coverage helped to focus the attention of the U.S. government on improving the security of its information. The press did not fully understand the level of sophistication of GUNMAN technology. They also did not appreciate the effort and talent used to discover the bug.

The GUNMAN experience had many positive effects on the Agency. NSA elements shared information and worked more cooperatively. The COMSEC organization gained a deeper appreciation of the ingenuity of the Soviets and thus a greater understanding of the threat to U.S. communications. GUNMAN demonstrated that the Soviets could be extraordinarily innovative and technologically sophisticated in their efforts to gain intelligence from U.S. diplomatic facilities. More Agency personnel gained expertise in reverse engineering, and there was a greater appreciation of the benefits of these techniques. NSA placed greater emphasis on the development of anti-tamper solutions to protect equipment, and customers were more interested in using these technologies. NSA learned valuable lessons from the enemy.

As a result of GUNMAN, NSA gained a stronger reputation as an expert in technical security within the U.S. government. Consequently, NSA was called upon to evaluate facilities and to provide advice to other segments of the government.

The GUNMAN incident had the greatest impact on the Department of State. Because of GUNMAN and other security problems, the State Department developed better security policies and procedures, especially in the areas of inspection and shipment of equipment. These practices are still in effect today.

GUNMAN did not have as much of an impact on the rest of the intelligence community. Individual agencies upgraded their own technical security efforts, but there was only limited progress in working cooperatively or sharing information.

GUNMAN led to a great flurry of investigations in which the U.S. attempted to learn from the Soviets. The question was not did we learn from the enemy, but how long will the U.S. government and the intelligence community remember the lessons that they learned from the GUNMAN project?

Although the GUNMAN discovery occurred almost thirty years ago and the Soviet Union was dissolved in 1991, the GUNMAN story is still relevant for the intelligence community. GUNMAN illustrated what can happen when we underestimate the capabilities of an adversary. It also highlighted the need for vigilance in maintaining security.

Acknowledgments

I wish to acknowledge the men and women of NSA who graciously and enthusiastically described their experience with Project GUNMAN. I also appreciated their patience and willingness to explain technical details of the project. This publication would not have been possible without their assistance.

I also wish to acknowledge the NSA Historian and the editorial staff of the Center for Cryptologic History for their guidance and assistance. They greatly enhanced the clarity and readability of the manuscript.

Notes

1. Transcript, *CBS Nightly News*. March 25, 1985.

2. George F. Kennan, *Memoirs: 1950 to 1963*. (New York, N.Y.: Pantheon Books, 1972), 152-157.

3. Transcript, *CBS Nightly News*. March 25, 1985.

4. The COMSEC Organization, NSA, A Special Report to the U.S. Congress: Project GUNMAN. March 1985, "Background." (NSA Archives, accession number 48399)

5. "Project GUNMAN: After the Smoke Cleared." November 1986, 7-8. (NSA Archives, accession number 46286)

6. Oral History 1998-17; LTG Lincoln D. Faurer; Interviewer: Tom Johnson. (Center for Cryptologic History)

7. Oral History 1996-34; Interviewer: Tom Johnson. (Center for Cryptologic History)

8. Oral History 1998-14; Interviewer: Tom Johnson. (Center for Cryptologic History)

9. "Project GUNMAN: After the Smoke Cleared." November 1986, 10-11.

10. S65 COMSEC Standards and Advanced Technology Division, Evaluation of Project GUNMAN, 28 January 1985. (NSA Archives, accession number 49509)

11. "Project GUNMAN: After the Smoke Cleared." November 1986, 14

12. The COMSEC Organization, NSA, A Special Report to the U.S. Congress: Project GUNMAN, March 1985, "Background."

13. Oral History 1998-14

14. Oral History 2007-20, Interviewers: Linda Murdock and Sharon Maneki. (Center for Cryptologic History)

15. Oral History 2007-29; Interviewers: Linda Murdock and Sharon Maneki. (Center for Cryptologic History)

16. Oral History 2006-38; Interviewers: Linda Murdock and Sharon Maneki. (Center for Cryptologic History)

17. Oral History 2007-06; Interviewers: Linda Murdock and Sharon Maneki (Center for Cryptologic History)

18. S65 COMSEC Standards and Advanced Technology Division, Evaluation of Project GUNMAN. 28 January 1985.

19. Oral History 2006-17; Interviewers: Linda Murdock and Sharon Maneki (Center for Cryptologic History)

20. Telephone conversation with Sharon Maneki, 18 December 2006

21. Oral History 1998-14

22. Oral History 2007-07; Interviewers: Linda Murdock and Sharon Maneki. (Center for Cryptologic History)

23. Oral History 2006-17

24. Oral History 2007-07

25. Oral History 2006-17

26. Oral History 2007-07

27. Oral History 2006-17

28. Oral History 2007-06

29. TEMPEST is a codename referring to investigations and studies of compromising emanations. These are defined as unintentional intelligence-bearing signals which, if intercepted and analyzed, disclose the information transmitted, received, handled, or otherwise processed by any information-processing equipment.

30. Oral History 2006-09; Interviewers: Linda Murdock and Sharon Maneki (Center for Cryptologic History)

31. Oral History 1998-15; Interviewer: Tom Johnson (Center for Cryptologic History)

32. Oral History 2006-09

33. Oral History 2006-47; Interviewers: Linda Murdock and Sharon Maneki (Center for Cryptologic History)

34. S65 COMSEC Standards and Advanced Technology Division, Evaluation of Project GUNMAN. 28 January 1985.

35. "Twelfth Interim Analysis Report on the GUNMAN Find." 18 October 1984.

36. "Thirteenth Interim Analysis Report on the GUNMAN Find." 25 October 1984.

37. "Sixth Interim Analysis Report on the GUNMAN Find." 6 September 1984.

38. "First Interim Analysis Report on the GUNMAN Find." no date.

39. Oral History 2009-03; Interviewers: David Cooley and Sharon Maneki (Center for Cryptologic History)

40. *Discover*, June 1985, "Tapping the Keys."

41. Oral History 2006-47

42. Oral History 2008-79; Interviewers: David Cooley and Sharon Maneki (Center for Cryptologic History)

43. *Time*, 8 April 1985, "A Deadly Serious Game."

44. "GUNMAN Text Recovery from IBM Selectric III Typewriters." C Expository Report No.18-91, 19 July 1991. (NSA Archives, accession number 49509)

45. "Parting Shot: Espionage Russia." (Federal Bureau of Investigation) March 15, 1985, 2 (NSA Archives, accession number 49509)

46. "Project GUNMAN: After the Smoke Cleared." November 1986, 19-21.

47. "The Legacy of GUNMAN" (briefing to the NSA workforce), 1 November 2000. (NSA Archives, accession number 49509)

48. "Parting Shot: Espionage Russia." (Federal Bureau of Investigation) March 15, 1985, 10 (NSA Archives, accession number 49509)

49. Ronald Kessler, *Moscow Station: How the KGB Penetrated the American Embassy*. (New York, NY: Macmillan Publishing Co. 1989), 97.

50. Oral History 1998-15

51. J. Craig Barker, *The Protection of Diplomatic Personnel*, Chapter 1. (Burlington, Vermont: Ashgate Publishing Co., 2006).

52. "Project GUNMAN: After the Smoke Cleared." November 1986, 23-25.

53. Oral History 2007-18; Interviewers: Linda Murdock and Sharon Maneki (Center for Cryptologic History)

54. Oral History 2006-18; Interviewers: Linda Murdock and Sharon Maneki (Center for Cryptologic History)

55. "Project GUNMAN: After the Smoke Cleared." November 1986, 37.

56. Organization Audit Trail Database (OATS).

57. "Project GUNMAN: After the Smoke Cleared." November 1986, 41.

58. In 1985 a spy ring consisting of former Navy personnel John Walker, Jerry Whitworth, Arthur Walker, and Michael Walker were convicted of (or pled guilty to) charges of passing classified U.S. intelligence material to the Soviet Union from 1968 to 1985. The ring reportedly helped the Soviets decipher more than one million encrypted U.S. naval messages.

59. Oral History 2006-17 (e-mail attachment to transcript)

60. Organization Audit Trail Database (OATS).

61. Oral History 2007-27; Interviewers: Linda Murdock and Sharon Maneki (Center for Cryptologic History)

www.ingramcontent.com/pod-product-compliance
Lightning Source LLC
Chambersburg PA
CBHW060904050426
42453CB00010B/1566